6/17

CULINARY MATH

MATH 24/7

Banking Math

Business Math

Computer Math

Culinary Math

Fashion Math

Game Math

Shopping Math

Sports Math

Time Math

Travel Math

MATH 24/7

CULINARY MATH

HELEN THOMPSON

Mason Crest

Mason Crest
450 Parkway Drive, Suite D
Broomall, PA 19008
www.masoncrest.com

Printed in the United States of America.

First printing
9 8 7 6 5 4 3 2 1

Series ISBN: 978-1-4222-2901-9
ISBN: 978-1-4222-2905-7
ebook ISBN: 978-1-4222-8916-7

The Library of Congress has cataloged the
        hardcopy format(s) as follows:

        Library of Congress Cataloging-in-Publication Data

Thompson, Helen, 1957-
  Culinary math / Helen Thompson.
     pages cm. – (Math 24/7)
  Audience: 10.
  Audience: Grade 4 to 6.
  Includes index.
     ISBN 978-1-4222-2905-7 (hardcover) – ISBN 978-1-4222-2901-9 (series) –
ISBN 978-1-4222-8916-7 (ebook)
  1. Cooking–Mathematics–Juvenile literature. I. Title.
  TX652.5.T525 2014
  641.501'51–dc23
                        2013015662

Produced by Vestal Creative Services.
www.vestalcreative.com

Contents

INTRODUCTION

How would you define math? It's not as easy as you might think. We know math has to do with numbers. We often think of it as a part, if not the basis, for the sciences, especially natural science, engineering, and medicine. When we think of math, most of us imagine equations and blackboards, formulas and textbooks.

But math is actually far bigger than that. Think about examples like Polykleitos, the fifth-century Greek sculptor, who used math to sculpt the "perfect" male nude. Or remember Leonardo da Vinci? He used geometry—what he called "golden rectangles," rectangles whose dimensions were visually pleasing—to create his famous *Mona Lisa*.

Math and art? Yes, exactly! Mathematics is essential to disciplines as diverse as medicine and the fine arts. Counting, calculation, measurement, and the study of shapes and the motions of physical objects: all these are woven into music and games, science and architecture. In fact, math developed out of everyday necessity, as a way to talk about the world around us. Math gives us a way to perceive the real world—and then allows us to manipulate the world in practical ways.

For example, as soon as two people come together to build something, they need a language to talk about the materials they'll be working with and the object that they would like to build. Imagine trying to build something—anything—without a ruler, without any way of telling someone else a measurement, or even without being able to communicate what the thing will look like when it's done!

The truth is: We use math every day, even when we don't realize that we are. We use it when we go shopping, when we play sports, when we look at the clock, when we travel, when we run a business, and even when we cook. Whether we realize it or not, we use it in countless other ordinary activities as well. Math is pretty much a 24/7 activity!

And yet lots of us think we hate math. We imagine math as the practice of dusty, old college professors writing out calculations endlessly. We have this idea in our heads that math has nothing to do with real life, and we tell ourselves that it's something we don't need to worry about outside of math class, out there in the real world.

But here's the reality: Math helps us do better in many areas of life. Adults who don't understand basic math applications run into lots of problems. The Federal Reserve, for example, found that people who went bankrupt had an average of one and a half times more debt than their income—in other words, if they were making $24,000 per year, they had an average debt of $36,000. There's a basic subtraction problem there that should have told them they were in trouble long before they had to file for bankruptcy!

As an adult, your career—whatever it is—will depend in part on your ability to calculate mathematically. Without math skills, you won't be able to become a scientist or a nurse, an engineer or a computer specialist. You won't be able to get a business degree—or work as a waitress, a construction worker, or at a checkout counter.

Every kind of sport requires math too. From scoring to strategy, you need to understand math—so whether you want to watch a football game on television or become a first-class athlete yourself, math skills will improve your experience.

And then there's the world of computers. All businesses today—from farmers to factories, from restaurants to hair salons—have at least one computer. Gigabytes, data, spreadsheets, and programming all require math comprehension. Sure, there are a lot of automated math functions you can use on your computer, but you need to be able to understand how to use them, and you need to be able to understand the results.

This kind of math is a skill we realize we need only when we are in a situation where we are required to do a quick calculation. Then we sometimes end up scratching our heads, not quite sure how to apply the math we learned in school to the real-life scenario. The books in this series will give you practice applying math to real-life situations, so that you can be ahead of the game. They'll get you started—but to learn more, you'll have to pay attention in math class and do your homework. There's no way around that.

But for the rest of your life—pretty much 24/7—you'll be glad you did!

1
GROCERY MATH

Lamar goes to culinary school, where he is learning to be a chef. Today, he is planning a special meal for five of his friends. They will be celebrating a friend's birthday, so Lamar wants to have all his friend's favorite foods: macaroni and cheese, hamburgers, salad, and chocolate cake. Lamar has chosen recipes, he's checked to see what ingredients he already has on hand, and now he has made a grocery list.

Here's what he plans to buy:

1 pound of macaroni

1 pound of cheese

1 quart of milk

3 pounds of ground beef

1 head of lettuce

3 tomatoes

1 jar of ketchup

1 jar of mustard

1 dozen hamburger buns

5 pounds of flour

5 pounds of sugar

1 package of baking chocolate

1 dozen eggs

a can of baking powder

salt

a bottle of salad dressing

a bottle of vegetable oil

a pound of butter

confectioner's sugar

Lamar has been saving his money, and he has $55 he can spend on the meal. When he gets to the grocery store, he discovers the following prices:

macaroni: $.99 per pound
cheese: $3.69 per pound
milk: $1.53 per quart
ground beef: $1.75 per pound
lettuce: $1.15 per head
tomatoes: $2.50 per pound
ketchup: $1.87 per bottle
mustard: $0.99 per bottle
hamburger buns: $3.75 for six
flour: $3.10 for 5 pounds

sugar: $2.95 for 5 pounds
baking chocolate: $4.75 per package
eggs: $2.99 per dozen
baking powder: $3.19 per can
salt: $2.10 per container
salad dressing: $2.75
cooking oil: $3.25 per bottle
butter: $2.80 per pound
confectioner's sugar: $2.15 per bag

How much will all this cost?

To find out, you'll need to add up the costs of each item. First, though, multiply wherever you need to.

If Lamar needs 3 pounds of ground beef, you'll need to multiply the cost for 1 pound by 3:

$$1.75 \times 3 =$$

If Lamar needs a dozen buns, you'll need to multiply the cost of 6 buns by 2:

$$3.75 \times 2 =$$

If he needs 3 tomatoes, he needs to know how much they will weigh. The average tomato weighs about 4 ounces, which means that 4 tomatoes weigh about a pound (16 ounces). Lamar only wants 3 tomatoes, though. So you will need to find the answer to this equation:

$$\tfrac{3}{4} \times 2.50 =$$

Now you need to add up everything.
Does Lamar have enough money?
Does he have any left over?
If so, how much?
And if not, how much more money does he need?

2
ESTIMATING AT THE GROCERY STORE

Once Lamar gets to the grocery store, he decides he'd like to make a fruit salad too. He picks up some bananas and strawberries. And the peppers look good to him as well; he wants to include them in the tossed salad.

But he's not sure he'll have enough money. The bananas cost 79 cents, the strawberries cost $3.89, and the peppers cost 33 cents each. He doesn't have a calculator with him to add up the amounts like you just did, and it's too many numbers for him to do in his head.

So how can Lamar avoid a nasty surprise when he gets to the checkout counter? He doesn't want to wait in line only to find out that he doesn't have enough money with him to pay for his groceries!

Estimating in your head is the way to have a good idea how much you are spending on groceries. You do that by rounding up to nearest dollar amount.

Fill out the chart on the next page. The first two entries have been done for you. When you're done, you'll be able to see whether Lamar can afford to buy the additional groceries.

ITEM	PRICE PER UNIT	YOUR ESTIMATE	RUNNING TOTAL
2 lbs. macaroni	$0.99 per lb	$2.00	$2.00
1 lb cheese	$3.69 per lb	$4.00	$6.00
1 qt milk	$1.53 per qt		
3 lbs ground beef	$1.75 per lb		
3 tomatoes (3/4 lb)	$2.50 per lb		
bottle of ketchup	$1.87 per bottle		
jar of mustard	$0.99 per jar		
dozen buns	$3.75 for 6		
5 lbs flour	$3.10 for 5 lbs		
5 lbs sugar	$2.95 for 5 lbs		
baking chocolate	$4.75 per package		
Eggs	$2.99 per dozen		
baking powder	$3.19 per can		
Salt	$2.10 per container		
salad dressing	$2.75 per bottle		
cooking oil	$3.25 per bottle		
1 lb butter	$2.80 per lb		
confectioner's sugar	$2.15 per bag		
Bananas	$0.79 per bunch		
Strawberries	$3.89 per package		
Peppers	$0.33 each		

Does Lamar have enough money?

3
GROCERY SHOPPING WITH COUPONS

While Lamar is shopping, he runs into his friend Kaylee, who is also doing some shopping. Kaylee has some coupons with her that she shares with Lamar. Now he won't have to spend quite so much money when he goes through the line.

Coupons are usually printed in newspapers and magazines. You'll need to cut out the coupons and bring them with you to the store. Sometimes you can find them online too, and then you'll need to print them up. Give your coupons to the cashier when you pay for the item, and she'll take off some money for that item.

How much money will Lamar save if he uses the coupons on the next page?

Percent means out of 100, so 25 percent means 25 out of 100. That's the same thing as one-fourth. (You can remember this, if you think about quarters, which equal 25 cents each—and there are 4 quarters in a dollar.) So if something is 25% off, that means that first you need to find out what one-fourth of the price is. You can do that by dividing the cost of butter by 4—and then subtracting that number from the cost.

Your equation will look like this:

$$\$2.80 - (\$2.80 \div 4) =$$

(Remember that you always do the part of the problem that's inside parentheses first.)

50% is the same thing as 50 out of 100—and that's the same thing as one-half. An easy way to find out how much something will cost if it's 50% off, is to find out how much it would cost if you took away one-half of the price. In this case, if you divide the cost of salt by 2, you'll know how much Lamar will have to spend on salt with the coupon.

20% means 20 out of 100. How many times does 20 go into 100?

Once you know that, you'll know the number to divide the cost of flour by.

And then you subtract that number from the cost.

What's your answer?

There's also another way you can figure out percents: you can use decimals. To do this, you'll need to remember that you have to move the decimal point two places. So 20% = .20. Then you can multiply the cost of flour by .20 (3.10 x .20), and you'll find out what 20% equals. Then you subtract that amount from $3.10 to find out what 20% off equals.

Either way you do it, you'll get the same answer. Use whichever way is easier for you to do in your head.

How much will Lamar save altogether if he uses all 3 coupons?

13

4

KITCHEN MEASUREMENTS

Now that Lamar has bought all his groceries, he's ready to start preparing the food. He lines up the groceries on the kitchen counter and gets out his recipes. The recipes, though, call for measurements that aren't listed on the food packages. He'll need to be able to convert from one unit of measurement to another in order to be sure he used the right amount of ingredients.

If you use the chart on the following page, you should be able to convert one kind of measurement into another fairly easily. You will need to multiply or divide to find the correct answers.

1 cup of grated cheese = 8 ounces
3 teaspoons = 1 tablespoon   16 tablespoons = 1 cup
1 cup = 8 ounces = 1/2 pint   2 cups = 16 ounces = 1 pint
4 cups = 32 ounces = 2 pints = 1 quart   2 quarts = 64 ounces = ½ gallon
4 quarts = 128 ounces = 1 gallon   1 square of baking chocolate = 1 ounce
1 stick of butter = 8 tablespoons = ½ cup = 4 ounces

1. Lamar's macaroni and cheese recipe calls for 8 ounces of grated cheese. How many cups will he need?

2. If the recipe needs 1½ cups of milk, how many ounces is that?

3. The recipe asks for ¼ cup of butter. How much of a stick of butter will that be? How many tablespoons will it be?

4. Lamar's recipe for chocolate cake calls for 16 ounces of flour. How many cups is that?

5. The cake needs 4 ounces of baking chocolate. How many squares will that be?

6. If Lamar needs 3 tablespoons of baking powder, how many teaspoons will that be?

7. How many cups will give him 2 quarts of water?

5
FRACTIONS IN THE KITCHEN

Recipes usually tell you how many servings they make. But sometimes you need to make a different number of servings. When that happens, you must adjust the amount of each ingredient in the recipe. Especially when you're making baked goods, you can't just throw in extra of one ingredient and expect the food to turn out right. Recipes for cakes, cookies, and breads are like chemical formulas: you need to keep the amounts exactly right or the cake, cookies, or bread won't rise right. It might turn out flat and hard—or it might rise too much and be full of bubbles.

So if you want to double a recipe you need to multiply each ingredient by 2. And if you want to make half of a recipe, you'll need use exactly half of each ingredient. You'll find some examples on the next page.

If you want to double a recipe that calls for 2½ cups of flour, first you will need to make improper fractions:

$$2 = \frac{2}{1}$$
$$2\frac{1}{2} = \frac{5}{2}$$

Then multiply them together:

$$\frac{2}{1} \times \frac{5}{2} = \frac{10}{2} = 5$$

So now you know you need 5 cups of flour to double the recipe.

This time suppose a recipe calls for 3½ cups of flour, but you want to make only half of the recipe. This time you will multiply by ½. When you turn 3 ½ into an improper fraction, you get ⁷⁄₂. So:

$$\frac{1}{2} \times \frac{7}{2} = \frac{7}{4} = 1\frac{3}{4}$$

So to make half the recipe, you will need 1¾ cups of flour.

An easy way to get the same answers is to remember these rules:

Double Recipe: To get twice as many servings, multiply the amount of each ingredient by 2.
Half Recipe: To get half the servings, divide the amount of each ingredient by 2.

But remember, if you're working with fractions, you'll need to turn them into improper fractions first before you multiply!

Now see if you can figure out the answers to these questions:

1. What about if a recipe makes 4 servings—but you need 12 servings? Will you need to multiply the numbers in the recipe or divide? What number will you use?

2. What if the recipe makes 15 servings, but you only want to make 5. Will you need to multiply or divide? What number will you use?

6
RECIPE MATH

Lamar is making macaroni and cheese for his friends. He wants to be able to serve 6 people and have enough for everyone to have one helping—but the recipe he's using only makes 4 servings. What will Lamar need to do?

This is a little more tricky. He needs his recipe to make ½ more than it does. So first he'll need to divide each ingredient amount by 2. And then he'll need to add that amount to the original amount.

On the next page, change the recipe so that it will make 6 servings instead of 4. The first ingredient has been done for you.

4 servings	+ ½ of 4	= 6 servings
1 package of macaroni	+ ½ package	= 1½ packages of macaroni
2 eggs		
2 cups milk		
2 tablespoons melted butter		
2½ cups shredded cheese		

On second thought, though, Lamar decides he wants to have enough macaroni and cheese so that everyone can have second helpings. This means he will need 12 servings instead. Can you fill out the chart below, changing the amount of ingredients so that this time he will end up with 12 servings?

4 servings	x 3	= 12 servings
1 package of macaroni	x 3	= 3 packages of macaroni
2 eggs		
2 cups milk		
2 tablespoons melted butter		
2½ cups shredded cheese		

7
MORE RECIPE MATH

Lamar also needs to bake the chocolate cake. He's decided to invite more people to drop by for dessert, so he wants to be sure the cake is big enough to serve 20 people. The recipe he wants to use, though, will only serve 8. How can he figure out how to make a cake big enough for that many people?

He has a couple of options. He could divide 20 by 8, which equals 2 with a remainder of 4. Since 4 is half of 8, this is the same thing as 2½.

$$20 \div 8 = 2½$$

Now he will need to multiply each of the ingredients in his recipe by 2½.

But Lamar wants to make it easier for himself. He decides to triple the recipe instead. This means he will multiply all the measurements by 3 instead. Multiplying by a whole number is easier.

Now he can cut the cake into slightly bigger slices and still have enough for everyone. Or he can have 4 pieces left over to keep for himself!

Fill in the chart on the next page to find out the amounts he'll need for each ingredient if he triples the recipe.

Original Cake Recipe	Tripled
1 cup flour	
1 cup sugar	
3 square baking chocolate	
1 teaspoons baking powder	
¾ teaspoons baking soda	
½ teaspoon salt	
½ cup milk	
¼ cup vegetable oil	
1 egg	
1 teaspoon vanilla extract	
½ cup boiling water	
1 cup all-purpose flour	
1 cup sugar	

Now Lamar will need to be sure he has enough frosting to cover the cake. He probably won't need exactly 3 times as much, but the cake will be bigger, so he's going to need more frosting. He decides to double the frosting recipe. Can you find the amounts he'll need?

Original Frosting Recipe	Doubled
1½ cups butter	
1 cup cocoa	
5 cups confectioner's sugar	
½ cup milk	
2 teaspoons vanilla extract	

How many sticks of butter will Lamar need now for the frosting? Look back to page 17 if you need to.

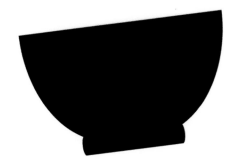

8
COOKING IN BATCHES

Lamar has a small grill on his deck where he is going to cook the hamburgers. However, the grill will only hold 4 burgers at a time. If Lamar wants to make enough burgers for each person to have 2, he'll need 12 burgers because he's expecting 6 people. This means he'll need to cook a batch at a time.

How many batches will he need?

$$12 \div 4 = 3$$

He'll need to make 3 batches.

If he wants to make enough for everyone to have 3 burgers, how many batches will he need to make?

Now Lamar realizes that it's going to take him a while to make that many batches of burgers. He's going to need to allow time for all the batches to cook.

If it takes 8 minutes for one batch to cook, how long will it take for him to cook 3 batches?

If he makes 18 burgers, enough for everyone to have 3, how long will he need to allow for the cooking time?

PRACTICES WITH BATCHES

Fill out the following chart for more practice.

	How Many Batches?	Cooking Time
You want to make 8 pieces of toast, but your toaster will only hold 2 slices of bread at a time. It takes 3 minutes for each batch to toast.		
You're baking cookies that need 12 minutes to bake. The recipe will make 36 cookies, but your cookie sheet will only hold 12 cookies at a time.		

9

USING TIME
IN THE KITCHEN

Lamar's friend George stops and says he will help Lamar get the food ready. Lamar asks George to cut up the tomatoes for the salad—but George works so slowly that Lamar is worried the tomatoes will never be cut. Lamar takes a deep breath and looks at the clock to figure out how much time he has.

It's 4:00 now, and his friends will be arriving at 6:30. That means he still has two and a half more hours to get ready.

The macaroni and cheese is made and it's ready to go in the oven. The cake is also made and ready to be baked, but he can't fit both the cake and the macaroni in the oven at the same time (and besides, they need different temperatures).

Here are the things Lamar still needs to do, with how much time each will take.

Task to Be Done	Time It Will Take
Bake the cake	35 minutes
Cool the cake	10 minutes
Make the frosting	10 minutes
Ice the cake	10 minutes
Bake the macaroni and cheese	45 minutes
Make the tossed salad	10 minutes
Make the fruit salad	10 minutes
Set the table	10 minutes
Grill the burgers	24 minutes

If Lamar does each one of these things, one at a time, how much time will it take?

Will he be done before his guests arrive?

The good news is—while things that need to go in the oven are baking, Lamar and George can be doing other tasks!

Lamar decides it makes sense to grill the hamburgers last, so they'll be as hot as possible. He decides to bake the cake first, so that it will have time to cool before he frosts it.

So if Lamar bakes the cake first, then puts the macaroni and cheese into the oven as soon as the cake comes out, what time will the macaroni and cheese be ready to come out of the oven?

While the cake and the macaroni are baking, will Lamar and George have time to do the other things they need to do?

10
LIQUID MATH

Lamar's friend Rashelle drops by and offers to help him and George prepare the meal. She's brought a few other things with her to add to the meal: a package of oatmeal cookies because Kaylee doesn't like chocolate and several bottles of soda and juice. She and Lamar decide to make punch by combining the soda and juice.

Rashelle brought 5 ten-ounce bottles of ginger ale, 2 gallon jugs of cranberry juice, and a half-gallon of apple juice. If she combines these altogether, how many cup servings will she have?

Look back to page 17 to fill out this chart.

	How Many Cups?
5 ten-ounce bottles of soda =	
2 gallons of cranberry juice =	
½ gallon of apple juice =	
TOTAL	

WHAT ABOUT METRIC?

Metric measurements are another way to measure liquids.

1 gallon = 3.8 liters

1 quart = .9 liters

1 cup = .2 liters

11
NUTRITION MATH

When Lamar's friend Ritesh arrives, he wants to find out how nutritious the meal will be. Ritesh is also going to culinary school, but he's focusing more on nutrition. He explains to his friends that everybody needs a balance of different nutrients in their diets. Rashelle wants to know how fattening their meal will be, and if the foods are healthy ones. Ritesh explains that calories, fat, salt, and sugar are all important factors in how healthy a particular food is. Unsaturated fat is better for you than saturated, he says. He pulls out his laptop and goes to a website that lets him type in different foods to find out their nutritional values.

The results he gets are shown below. Most of these numbers are given in grams and milligrams. One gram weighs about as much as paperclip. A milligram is lighter, and weighs about the same as a snowflake.

1 Serving	Calories	Sugar	Fat	Saturated Fat	Sodium (Salt)
macaroni & cheese	200	1 g	6 g	2 g	1027 mg
hamburger	230	0 g	15 g	6 g	64 mg
tossed salad	25	0 g	0 g	0 g	0 mg
fruit salad	50	7 g	0 g	0 g	0 mg
punch	150	36 g	0 g	0 g	0 mg
chocolate cake	236	32 g	10 g	3 g	214 mg

1. How many calories are in Lamar's meal, if his friends only eat one serving?
2. What about if they eat two servings?
3. How much sugar (in grams) is in one serving of the meal? How does this compare to the recommended daily requirement shown in the chart below?
4. Sodium is another name for salt. How much salt (in milligrams) is in one serving of this meal?
5. How healthy do you think this meal is when it comes to calories, fat, sugar, and salt?

Daily Diet Reccomendations:

	Men	Women	Children 4-8	Boys 9-13	Boys 14-18	Girls 9-13	Girls 14-18
Fat	20–35% of daily calories	20–35% of daily calories	25–35% of daily calories	25–35% of daily calories	25–35% of daily calories	25–35% of daily calories	25–25% of daily calories
Saturated Fat	less than 10% of daily calories	less than 10% of daily calories	less than 10% of daily calories	less than 10% of daily calories	less than 10% of daily calories	less than 10% of daily calories	less than 10% of daily calories
Sodium	less than 2300 mg	less than 2300 mg	less than 1900 mg	less than 2200 mg	less than 2300 mg	less than 2200 mg	less than 2300 mg
Sugar	37.5 grams	25 grams	12 grams	12 grams	12 grams	12 grams	12 grams

Sources: U.S. Food and Drug Administration and the American Heart Association.

12
GREATER THAN AND LESS THAN: FOOD LABEL MATH

Rashelle points out that Ritesh left out the salad dressing when he was looking up things online. Before Ritesh can open up his laptop again, Lamar tells his friends that a lot of foods come with labels that tell you how many nutrients it has and if it's healthy or not. Foods like salad dressing that come in bottles or other foods in boxes or bags have labels that give lots of nutrition information.

You'll find food labels on just about every food with a package. Look for a black and white chart with a whole bunch of numbers. You need 100 percent of every nutrient every day to be at your healthiest. Daily values tell you how close you are to getting 100 percent of each nutrient.

Nutrition Facts

Serving Size 2 Tbsp (30g)
Servings Per Container about 12
Calories 70
   Calories from Fat 50
*Percent Daily Values are based on a 2.000 calorie diet.

Amount / Serving	% Daily Value*	Amount / Serving	% Daily Value*
Total Fat 6g	9%	**Total Carbohydrate** 3g	1%
Saturated Fat 3.5g	18%	Dietary Fiber 0g	0%
Trans Fat 0g		Sugars 2g	
Cholesterol 20mg	7%	**Protein** 1g	
Sodium 180mg	7%		
Vitamin A 6% • Vitamin C 2%		Calcium 4% • Iron 0%	

Compare the salad dressing food label above with the food label below from the cookies that Rashelle brought. Insert either < or > into each blank below:

1. Which food has more fat per serving?

salad dressing _____ cookies

2. Which food has more calories per serving?

salad dressing _____ cookies

3. Which one has more salt?

salad dressing _____ cookies

4. Which one has more sugar per serving?

salad dressing _____ cookies

How healthy do you think these foods are? Should people who want a healthy diet eat a lot of them? Why or why not?

Nutrition Facts

Serving Size 1 Cookie (17g)
Servings Per Container About 12
Calories 80
   Calories from Fat 40
*Percent Daily Values are based on a 2,000 calorie diet.

Amount / Serving	% Daily Value*	Amount / Serving	% Daily Value*
Total Fat 4.5g	7%	**Total Carbohydrate** 7g	2%
Saturated Fat 2.5g	13%	Dietary Fiber 1g	4%
Trans Fat 0g		Sugars 4g	
Cholesterol 5mg	2%	**Protein** 1g	
Sodium 20mg	1%		
Vitamin A 0% • Vitamin C 0%		Calcium 0% • Iron 2%	

13
COUNTING
CALORIES

Ritesh explains to his friends that there's a connection between different kinds of nutrients and the number of calories in foods.

"Our bodies need different nutrients from the food we eat," Ritesh says. "We need a balance of **protein**, **carbohydrates**, and fat. We need protein to keep our muscles healthy. We need carbohydrates for energy. And we need healthy fat to help us absorb vitamins and for energy."

We get protein from meat and dairy products, like cheese and milk. Carbohydrates are in breads, desserts, fruits, and vegetables. Fat is found in meat and dairy products, as well as in many snacks. Each kind of nutrient has a different number of calories.

Protein, for example, is a nutrient that has 4 calories in every gram. If you were eating some cheese with 7 grams of protein, you would be eating 28 calories that came from protein.

7 grams protein x 4 calories per gram = 28 calories

Other calories in the cheese come from other nutrients.

Carbohydrates also have four calories per gram. Soda, for example, has a lot of sugar, which is a carbohydrate. One can of soda usually has around 40 grams of sugar. In all, there are 160 calories from that sugar.

40 grams sugar x 4 calories per gram = 160 calories

Soda doesn't really have anything else in it, so all the calories in it come from sugar.

Fat has the most calories per gram. Fat has 9 calories for every gram. Half an avocado has about eleven grams of healthy, unsaturated fat. When you do the math, you see half an avocado has 99 calories.

11 grams of fat x 9 calories per gram = 99 calories

Look back on page 29 to answer these questions:

1. How many calories come from fat in a serving of macaroni and cheese?
2. How many calories come from sugar in chocolate cake?

Now look at the food labels on page 31 to answer these questions:

3. How many calories come from protein in one cookie?
4. How many calories come from fat in serving of salad dressing?

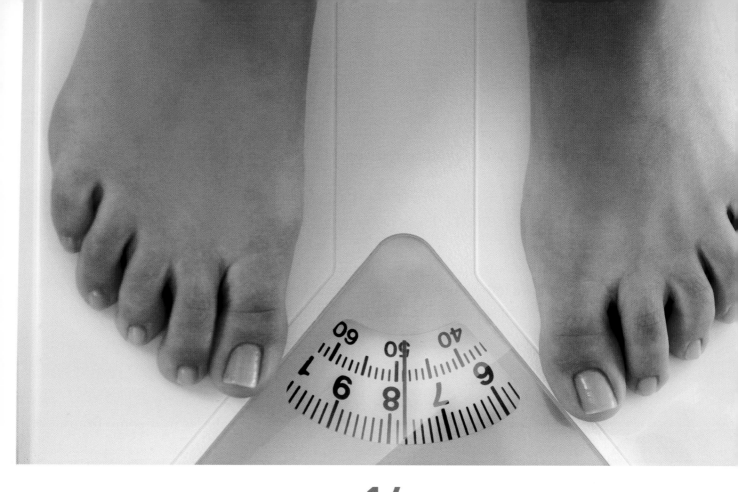

14

HOW MANY CALORIES DO YOU NEED?

While Lamar and his friends eat the meal he prepared, they laugh and have a good time. After dinner, Kaylee and George offer to clean up the kitchen, while the others hang out in the living room.

As they are putting the dishes in the dishwasher, they talk some more about calories. George tells Kaylee he's worried he may be overweight and wonders if he should go on a diet. Kaylee explains to him that you can't just stand on the scales to tell whether you weigh too much. Everyone's body is different. Some people have heavier bones. Some have more muscle. Some are tall, short, and everything in between.

Doctors have come up with a way to tell if people weigh too much. They call it the Body Mass Index, or BMI. BMI depends on how tall you are and how much you weigh. It's a number. Everyone has a BMI. Your BMI can tell you if you're overweight or obese—or if you're underweight or just right. Most people need about 2,000 calories a day. If you're overweight, then you should cut back on your calories to lose weight. If you're underweight, though, you might need to eat more calories.

BMI FORMULA

If you want to figure out your own BMI, here's what you need to do:

1. Weigh yourself and write it down.
2. Measure how tall you are in inches (height) and write it down.
3. Use this equation.

$$\text{Weight} \div (\text{height} \times \text{height}) \times 703$$

4. If you're under age 20, though, other factors will affect your BMI. Go to the U.S. government's Centers for Disease Control and Prevention (CDC) website at apps.nccd. cdc.gov/dnpabmi. You'll be able to plug in your measurements there to calculate your BMI.

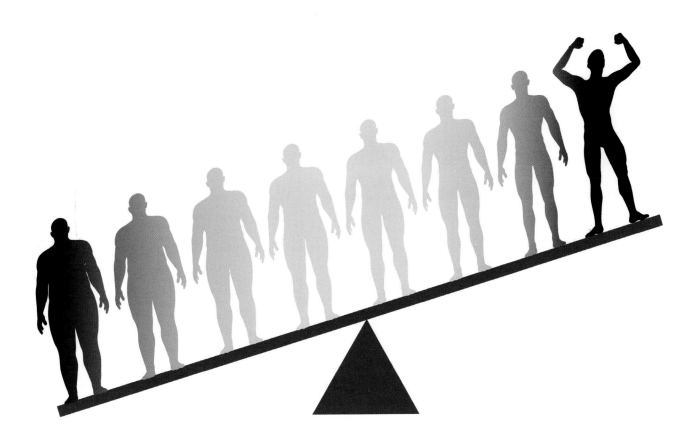

15
PUTTING IT ALL TOGETHER

Now that all the cooking is done, Lamar feels pretty proud of himself that he was able to pull off the meal so well—math and all.

See if you can remember all the math that went into this meal.

1. A bag of potato chips cost $1.99. You want to buy 5 bags. How much will they cost altogether?

2. You have $10 with you when you go to the store for groceries. You need to buy these things:

   milk: $1.88
   bread: $.99
   peanut butter: $3.87
   jelly: $2.89

   Estimate to find out if you have enough money with you. What about if you buy 2 loaves of bread? Will you still have enough?

3. You discover you have a coupon with you for the milk. The coupon is for 50% off. How much will the milk cost now?

4. Fill in the blanks below:

   5 cups = _____ ounces
   16 cups = _____ pints
   6 quarts = _____ gallons

5. A recipe calls for ¾ cup flour. You want to double the recipe. How much flour will you need now?

6. You can only fit 12 cookies at a time into the oven. You want to make 60 cookies. How many batches will you need to make?

7. If each batch of cookies takes 12 minutes to bake, how long will you need to bake all 60 cookies?

8. If a package of potato chips says it has 10 grams of fat per serving, how many calories do those 10 grams equal?

9. You add up all the calories you eat in a day, and find you ate 3,400 calories. If you eat like that every day, will you probably gain weight or lose weight?

FIND OUT MORE IN BOOKS

Blocker, Linda and Julia Hill. *Culinary Math*. Hoboken, N.J.: Wiley, 2007.

D'Amico, Joan and Karen Eich Drummond. *The Math Chef: Over 60 Math Activities and Recipes for Kids*. Hoboken, N.J.: Wiley, 2007.

McCallum, Ann. *Eat Your Math Homework: Recipes for Hungry Minds*. Watertown, Mass.: Charlesbridge, 2011.

Minden, Cecilia. *Grocery Shopping by the Numbers*. North Mankato, Minn.: Cherry Lake, 2007.

Nissenberg, Sandra. *The Everything Kids' Cookbook: From Mac n Cheese to Double Chocolate Chip Cookies—90 Recipes to Have some Finger-Lickin Fun*. Avon, Mass.: Adams Media, 2008.

Weiss, Ellen. *Math in the Kitchen*. Chicago, Ill.: Children's Press, 2007.

FIND OUT MORE
ON THE INTERNET

Calculate Your Body Mass Index
www.nhlbisupport.com/bmi

Cooking by Numbers
www.learner.org/interactives/dailymath/cooking.html

Cooking with Chef Piglet
www.knowledgeadventure.com/games/cooking-with-chef-piglet.aspx

Cooking with Math
mathcentral.uregina.ca/beyond/articles/Cooking/Cooking1.html

Grocery Store Math
momshomeroom.msn.com/parenting-videos/math/grocery-store-math/253

Math and Science Gumbo
www.youtube.com/watch?v=HA0kF6OJTVQ

Math Fun with Food Labels
blog.fooducate.com/2012/06/30/some-math-fun-with-nutriton-facts-labels

Want to Be Healthy? It Pays to Do the Math
www.thenutritionexperts.com/2009/02/want-to-be-healthy-it-pays-to-do-the-math

Glossary

Calories: a measure of how much energy is in food; one calorie equals the amount of energy it takes to raise a gram of water one degree Celsius.

Carbohydrates: nutrients humans need for energy; sugar, fiber, and starch are all carbohydrates.

Chef: someone who cooks for a living.

Convert: to change from one unit to another.

Culinary: referring to food preparation.

Ingredients: the individual foods that go into making a recipe.

Nutrients: substances we need for our bodies to work right, and which we must get through food.

Nutrition: all the ways we get and eat food.

Protein: a nutrient people need for healthy muscles and growth.

Recommended daily requirement: the amount of a nutrient scientists tell us we should eat every day.

Saturated: filled, containing the largest possible amount.

Unsaturated: not filled, able to contain more.

Answers

1.

1.75 x 3 = 5.25
3.75 x 2 = 7.5
¾ x 2.50 = 1.90

Does Lamar have enough money? Yes. He needs $54.90, and he has $55.
Does he have any left over? Yes.
If so, how much? He has ten cents left.
And if not, how much more money does he need? He has enough money.

2.

ITEM	PRICE PER UNIT	YOUR ESTIMATE	RUNNING TOTAL
2 lbs. macaroni	$0.99 per lb	$2.00	$2.00
1 lb cheese	$3.69 per lb	$4.00	$6.00
1 qt milk	$1.53 per qt	$2.00	$8.00
3 lbs ground beef	$1.75 per lb	$6.00	$14.00
3 tomatoes (3/4 lb)	$2.50 per lb	$2.00	$16.00
bottle of ketchup	$1.87 per bottle	$2.00	$18.00
jar of mustard	$0.99 per jar	$1.00	$19.00
dozen buns	$3.75 for 6	$8.00	$27.00
5 lbs flour	$3.10 for 5 lbs	$4.00	$31.00
5 lbs sugar	$2.95 for 5 lbs	$3.00	$34.00
baking chocolate	$4.75 per package	$5.00	$39.00
Eggs	$2.99 per dozen	$3.00	$42.00
baking powder	$3.19 per can	$4.00	$46.00
Salt	$2.10 per container	$3.00	$49.00
salad dressing	$2.75 per bottle	$3.00	$52.00
cooking oil	$3.25 per bottle	$4.00	$56.00
1 lb butter	$2.80 per lb	$3.00	$59.00
confectioner's sugar	$2.15 per bag	$3.00	$62.00
Bananas	$0.79 per bunch	$1.00	$63.00
Strawberries	$3.89 per package	$4.00	$67.00
Peppers	$0.33 each	$1.00	$68.00

Does Lamar have enough money? No. By rounding up to the nearest dollar, and adding in the fruit salad, Lamar needs $68 now.

3.

$2.80 – ($2.80 ÷ 4) = $2.10
20% means 20 out of 100. How many times does 20 go into 100? 5 times.
What's your answer? $3.10 – ($3.10 ÷ 5)= $2.48
How much will Lamar save altogether if he uses all 3 coupons? He's saving ($2.80 –$2.10) + ($2.10 – $1.05) + ($3.10 – $2.48) = $2.37 in savings.

4.

1. 1 cup
2. 12 ounces
3. ½ stick, 4 tablespoons
4. 2 cups
5. 4 squares
6. 9 teaspoons
7. 8 cups

5.

1. Multiply the numbers by 3.
2. Divide the numbers by 3.

6.

4 servings	+ ½ of 4	= 6 servings
1 package of macaroni	+ ½ package	= 1½ packages of macaroni
2 eggs	+ 1 egg	= 3 eggs
2 cups milk	+ 1 cup	= 3 cups
2 tablespoons melted butter	+ 1 tablespoon	= 3 tablespoons
2½ cups shredded cheese	+ 1 ¼ cup	= 3 ¾ cups

4 servings	x 3	= 12 servings
1 package of macaroni	x 3	= 3 packages of macaroni

2 eggs	x 3	= 6 eggs
2 cups milk	x 3	= 6 cups
2 tablespoons melted butter	x 3	= 6 tablespoons
2½ cups shredded cheese	x 3	= 7 ½ cups

7.

Original Cake Recipe	Tripled
1 cup flour	3 cups
1 cup sugar	3 cups
3 square baking chocolate	9 squares
1 teaspoons baking powder	3 teaspoons
3/4 teaspoons baking soda	2 ¼ teaspoons
½ teaspoon salt	1 ½ teaspoons
½ cup milk	1 ½ cups
¼ cup vegetable oil	¾ cup
1 egg	3 eggs
1 teaspoon vanilla extract	3 teaspoons
½ cup boiling water	1 ½ cups
1 cup all-purpose flour	3 cups
1 cup sugar	3 cups

Original Frosting Recipe	Doubled
1½ cups butter	3 cups
1 cup cocoa	2 cups
5 cups confectioner's sugar	10 cups
½ cup milk	1 cups
2 teaspoons vanilla extract	4 teaspoons

How many sticks of butter will Lamar need now for the frosting? 6 sticks.

8.

If he wants to make enough for everyone to have 3 burgers, how many batches will he need to make? 18 burgers divided by 4 burger per batch= 4 ½ batches

If it takes 8 minutes for one batch to cook, how long will it take for him to cook 3 batches? 8 minutes x 3 batches= 24 minutes

If he makes 18 burgers, enough for everyone to have 3, how long will he need to allow for the cooking time? $^{18}\!/_4$ x 8 = 36 minutes

	How Many Batches?	Cooking Time
You want to make 8 pieces of toast, but your toaster will only hold 2 slices of bread at a time. It takes 3 minutes for each batch to toast.	4 batches	12 minutes
You're baking cookies that need 12 minutes to bake. The recipe will make 36 cookies, but your cookie sheet will only hold 12 cookies at a time.	3 batches	36 minutes

9.

If Lamar does each one of these things, one at a time, how much time will it take? 164 minutes, or 2 hours and 44 minutes.

Will he be done before his guests arrive? Not quite. He only has 2 hours and 30 minutes.

So if Lamar bakes the cake first, then puts the macaroni and cheese into the oven as soon as the cake comes out, what time will the macaroni and cheese be ready to come out of the oven? 35 minutes + 45 minutes= 80 minutes from now.

While the cake and the macaroni are baking, will Lamar and George have time to do the other things they need to do? The other tasks will take 84 minutes to do, so they will just about have time.

10.

	How Many Cups?
5 ten-ounce bottles of soda =	6 ¼ cups
2 gallons of cranberry juice =	32 cups
½ gallon of apple juice =	8 cups
TOTAL	46 ¼ cups

11.

1. How many calories are in Lamar's meal, if his friends only eat one serving? 891 calories
2. What about if they eat two servings? 1782 calories.
3. How much sugar (in grams) is in one serving of the meal? How does this compare to the recommended daily requirement shown in the chart below? 76 grams. One serving has 64 more grams of sugar than the daily recommended value.
4. Sodium is another name for salt. How much salt (in milligrams) is in one serving of this meal? How does this compare to to the recommended daily requirement show in the chart below? 1305 milligrams. One serving has 1005 fewer calories than the recommended requirement.
5. How healthy do you think this meal is when it comes to calories, fat, sugar, and salt? This meal could be a lot healthier, because it has a lot of fat, sugar, and salt.

12.

1. >
2. <
3. >
4. <

How healthy do you think these foods are? Should people who want a healthy diet eat a lot of them? Why or why not? These foods aren't that healthy because they don't have a lot of good nutrients in them, but they do have some sugar, salt, and fat. People should limit how much they eat of them.

13.

1. How many calories come from fat in a serving of macaroni and cheese? 6 grams of fat x 9 calories per gram= 54 calories
2. How many calories come from sugar in chocolate cake? 32 grams of sugar x 4 calories per gram= 128 calories

Now look at the food labels on page 31 to answer these questions:

3. How many calories come from protein in one cookie? 1 gram of protein x 4 calories per gram= 4 calories

4. How many calories come from fat in serving of salad dressing? 6 grams of fat x 9 calories per gram= 54 calories.

15.

1. $1.99 x 5 = $9.95
2. You do have enough money. You won't have enough if you buy two loaves of bread.
3. $1.88 x .5 = $.94
4. 40, 8, 1 ½
5. 1 ½ cups
6. 60 ÷ 12 = 5 batches
7. 12 minutes x 5 = 60 minutes
8. 10 grams of fat x 9 calories per gram = 90 calories
9. You will gain weight, because you only need around 2,000 calories a day.

INDEX

About the Author

Helen Thompson lives in upstate New York. She worked first as a social worker and then became a teacher as her second career.

Picture Credits

Clkr.com: p. 27
Dreamstime.com:
    9am9pm: p. 33
    A J Cotton: p. 8, 10, 26, 36
    Andres Rodriguez: p. 34
    Brett Critchley: p. 20
    Christopher Smith: p. 22
    Dawn Hudson: p. 25
    Diana Valujeva: p. 24
    Elopaint: p. 11
    Helenlbuxton: p. 14
    Ivonne Wierink: p. 30
    Jovani Carlo Gorospe: p. 16
    Leerodney Avison: p. 32
    Licoricelegs: p. 28
    Michael Brown: p. 35
    P B: p. 18
    Patrimonio Designs Limited: p. 13
    Soleilc: p. 15, 17, 19, 21, 23
    Stephen Coburn: p. 12
    Trahcus: p. 27
    Vector: p. 9